each a glimpse...

© Colin T Gifford 2012

First published 2012
ISBN 978 0 7110 3529 4

Published by Ian Allan Publishing
an imprint of Ian Allan Publishing Ltd.,
Hersham, Surrey KT12 4RG
Printed in China

Distributed in the United States of America and Canada
by BookMasters Distribution Services

Visit the Ian Allan Publishing website at
www.ianallanpublishing.com

Ian Allan
PUBLISHING

and ever again...

Colin T Gifford

(i)
(ii) (iii)

(i) Tiverton
(ii) Goole
(iii) Darlington

© Colin T Gifford 2011
Designed by Colin T Gifford
Cover design and typography by Colin T Gifford
Produced by Colin T Gifford, David Postle and Adrian White
Computer origination by David Postle

By the same author
DECLINE OF STEAM
EACH A GLIMPSE . . . (First Edition)
. . . AND GONE FOREVER
STEAM FINALE NORTH
STEAM RAILWAYS IN INDUSTRY (with Horace Gamble)

courtesy N H Willoughby

preface

"Don't get under my feet!"
This pronouncement effectively meant 'go out to play' which in turn generally meant either messing around on a bomb-site, playing football or cricket in the street or strapping on roller-skates for a game of hockey in Offord Road. I was 10/11ish living in Islington a couple of years after the war and the railways were not yet nationalized.

Occasionally when nobody was 'out to play' I would skate through Chapel Market and down to the Euston Road for brief visits to its three main line termini with their inviting concourses – St Pancras had a wonderful slope outside, used by taxis, dropping down to the main road; Euston had a good surface but was more confined and less hospitable whereas King's Cross had the smoothest 'rink' and was the most accessible. If I was going to be hooked into collecting engine numbers then surely these visits would have been sufficient impetus; after all, Ian Allan's ABCs had been around for a couple of years and I knew a few 'train spotters'. But no, it was the place names and what I imagined they represented that appealed. Furtively I would glimpse the many luggage labels and note train announcements; Aberdeen, Edinburgh, Newcastle, Leeds, York and so on…for me evocative, mysterious, inviting, but unget-at-able places.

Ten years would elapse before I was in a position to begin to give substance to my imagined images. In 1957 I acquired the regular use of a Rolleiflex and initially followed the examples as perpetuated in the railway press wherein, for the most part, the locomotive and its train, photographed in sunshine, dominated. But within a few years, railways and trains in context had become my photographic objective. This of course meant a peopled, social, workaday environment through day and night and in all kinds of weather.

A similar transition, but to a lesser extent, has taken place in the field of railway photography and it is this broader approach, in conjunction with nostalgia and environmental changes during the last forty to fifty years, that has prompted this revision. Primarily the pictures that have 'more to say' have been given more space which ipso facto, within the defined extent of the book, has necessitated the elimination of others. However, in order to retain continuity and the theme aspect of the production, some new images have been included. What's next?

'…in the wink of an eye'
in glorious subdued colour.

123
4

1. 44891 leaves Bredbury for Newton Heath locomotive sheds, 3rd May, 1968.
2. The south end of platform 3 Crewe, 6th September, 1964.
3. Cabside of a "Caley Pug" at Inverness, 22nd July, 1959.
4. A southbound freight crosses the Lune at Lancaster, 9th June, 1965.

The Bootle Branch, Liverpool,
17th April, 1968

5. 44806 leaves the cattle station sidings at Stanley.
6. 48614 passes the site of Stanley station with an Edge Hill - Alexandra Dock freight.
7. 48206 with a Canada Dock - Edge Hill freight at Clubmoor recreation ground.

8. 44906 arrives with a freight at Liverpool Edge Hill upper reception and sorting sidings, 19th February, 1968.

9. An 8F 2.8.0 and northbound freight cross Stockport Viaduct beyond Mersey Square bus station, 2nd May, 1968.

10. 45739 'Ulster' leaves Accrington with a Leeds City - Blackpool North return excursion, 23rd July, 1966.

11. 45200 leaves Stockport Edgeley with a northbound parcels train, 20th March, 1961.

12. 45305 with a southbound freight on the viaduct approaching Runcorn station, 22nd November, 1967.

13. 65901 passes through Burntisland with West Highland bound tankers from the British Aluminium works, 1st October, 1966.
14. 44906 with a northbound parcels train at Oxenholme passes 42236, the Grayrigg banker, 27th February, 1967.
15. 48759 passes Frodingham Trent Jnc. with a westbound steel train, 30th October, 1965.

13

14 15

16. 69509 (right) on empty stock and 67608 with a train for Helensburgh at Bridgeton Central, Glasgow, 6th July, 1960.

17. 69188 with a parcels train and 67644 on a train for Kirkintilloch at Glasgow Queen Street, 8th July, 1960.

18. 60004 'William Whitelaw' leaves Queen Street, Glasgow, with an express for London Kings Cross, 18th July, 1961.

19. 42170 at Glasgow Central (Low Level) with a Kilbowie-Coatbridge Central train, 3rd July, 1963.

20. 69005, station pilot at Newcastle Central, with 67690 leaving on a parcels train for the Carlisle line, 24th December, 1958.

21. 49173 at Walsall with a Water Orton-Willenhall freight, 9th November, 1963.

Widnes, 8th February, 1968.

22. 92160 at Appleton with coal empties for St. Helens.
23. 48305 leaves Ditton with a freight for Folly Lane, Runcorn.
24. 45296 on the viaduct approach to Runcorn Bridge.

25. 48316 crosses the Bridgewater Canal at West Timperley bound for Partington, 11th December, 1966.
26. 75037 at Lambrigg working north to Tebay, 18th November, 1967.

25 26

27. 70022 'Tornado' with a Carlisle-Crewe parcels
train at Lambrigg, 18th November, 1967.
28. 44780 in the Lune Gorge with a northbound
freight, 18th November, 1967.
29. 70024 'Vulcan' and a northbound freight approach
Dillicar water troughs, 14th September, 1967.

27
28 29

30. A Class 5MT 4.6.0 leaves Tebay with a northbound freight
banked by Class 4 2.6.0, 29th November, 1967.
31. The following day sees a similar combination approaching
Shap Summit.

32. 44957 and 61343 on the Horseshoe Curve north of Tyndrum with a combined
Mallaig and Fort William - Glasgow Queen Street, Edinburgh Waverley and
London Kings Cross train, 20th July, 1961.
33. 8431 and 6602 climb out of Swansea Victoria with a Sunday school excursion
to Builth Road, 3rd June, 1964.

34. 8431 and 6602 topping the climb out of Swansea Victoria, 3rd June, 1964.
35. 48115 with Garston - Godley coal empties passes 92160 with coal from Godley to Garston at Brinnington Jnc., 4th May, 1968.
36. 34036 'Westward Ho' with an express from Waterloo to Bournemouth passes 73065 on a Basingstoke - Waterloo train at Clapham Junction, 20th May, 1965.

37. 45287 waits at Liverpool Lime Street to
return to Edge Hill MPD, 20th April, 1968.
38. 45282 approaches Stockport Tiviot Dale with a
westbound freight and passes 48356, the
Brinnington banker, shunting the
down sidings at Portwood, 3rd May, 1968.
39. 44962 with Liverpool-Leigh coal empties
approaches 48752, light engine, at Ince Moss,
Wigan, 23rd November, 1967.

40. 44732 leaves Wigan North Western for Blackpool South with a train from Crewe, 12th November, 1964.

41. 45318 and 48313 outside Bolton locomotive shed, 22nd August, 1967.

42. 47280 pulls out of Cockshute Sidings, Stoke with coal empties as 44946 passes Newcastle Jcn. box on the up main line, 9th November, 1964.

43. 47326, station pilot, at the north end of Carlisle Citadel, 10th June, 1964.
44. 42806 passes through Ardrossan Town with a northbound freight, 22nd June, 1962.
45. 31408 approaches Ash with a Redhill - Reading train, 2nd January, 1965.

46. 34038 'Lynton' approaches Farnborough with a Nine Elms - Southampton freight, 2nd January, 1965.
47. 34095 'Brentor' leaves Winchester with a Bournemouth - Waterloo express, 14th January, 1967.

48. 48307 and westbound coal train at Hebden Bridge, 30th May, 1967.
49. 42116 at Wortley West junction, Leeds, with the Bradford Exchange portion
of an express from Kings Cross, 17th September, 1966.

50. A Class 5MT 4.6.0 by Burscough Moss with a Liverpool Exchange - Glasgow Central express, 23rd November, 1967.

51. 45420 passes through Kirkdale, Liverpool, with the same service, 20th February, 1968.

52. 44800 leaves Preston with the Glasgow - Liverpool train, 18th February, 1968.

50 52
51

53 54

53. 45411 leaves Preston with a Glasgow Central-Manchester Victoria express, 11th January, 1968.
54. 7029 'Clun Castle' climbs Gresford bank with the "Zulu", one of two specials organised by Ian Allan Ltd.
to work between London Paddington and Birkenhead Woodside on 4th March, 1967.

55 56

55. 'Clun Castle' and the "Zulu" climb to Gresford, 4th March, 1967.
56. 4472 'Flying Scotsman', shortly after leaving Kings Cross with the 40th anniversary non-stop run
of the "Flying Scotsman" train, passes Belle Isle and under the North London line
alongside the regular Deltic-hauled "Flying Scotsman", 1st May, 1968.

57. 60002 'Sir Murrough Wilson', 60008 'Dwight D. Eisenhower' and 60029 'Woodcock'
at London Kings Cross, 07.30 Sunday 12th March, 1961.
58. 60007 'Sir Nigel Gresley' at Hatfield with a Kings Cross - Leeds Central relief,
22nd December, 1962.

57 58

59. 46247 'City of Liverpool' on a train for Perth at Carlisle Citadel, 14th October, 1961.
60. 46246 'City of Manchester' inside Carlisle Upperby roundhouse with 45632 'Tonga' behind, 30th September, 1961.
61. 46255 'City of Hereford' leaves Stirling at 20.35 and passes 45213 and 57261 on the locomotive shed with the car-sleeper to Sutton Coldfield, 3rd July, 1963.

59
60 61

62 64
63

62. 60898 at Bannockburn with the southbound "Grampian" from Aberdeen to Glasgow Buchanan Street station, 1st July, 1963.
63. 64569 leaves Markinch with a freight for Thornton Junction, 28th September, 1966.
64. 45115 arrives at Stranraer Harbour, terminus of its train from Dumfries, 11th June, 1965.

65. 84025 with the auto-train to Chorley
at Horwich terminus, 8th June, 1965.
66. Art class at Seacombe Junction, Bidston,
17th July, 1967.
67. 73022 at Raynes Park with an Eastleigh - Waterloo
train, 6th April, 1965.

68. 35008 'Orient Line' leaves Southampton with a Waterloo - Bournemouth express, 4th February, 1967.
69. 65879 at Ryhope with a Silksworth - Sunderland South Dock coal train, 31st August, 1967.
70. No. 18 'Ningwood' near Medina Wharf with a Cowes - Ryde train, 7th August, 1965.

68
69 70

71. No.29 'Alverstone' crosses the Medina at the south end of Newport station, Isle of Wight, with a train from Cowes to Ryde Pier Head, 16th October, 1965.
72. No.14 'Fishbourne' leaves the north end of the station with a Ryde – Cowes train, 17th October, 1965.

71 72

Newport, Monmouthshire, Sunday 7th April, 1963

73. 5091 'Cleeve Abbey' leaves Hillfield Tunnel with a Manchester Piccadilly - Swansea High Street express.
74. 5942 'Doldowlod Hall' crosses the Usk with a Cardiff General - Manchester Piccadilly train.
75. 7929 'Wyke Hall' in the station on empty stock as 5014 'Goodrich Castle' passes with an eastbound freight.

76. 6909 'Frewin Hall' in Birmingham Snow Hill with a Leamington Spa - Wolverhampton Low Level parcels train, 10th April, 1964.
77. 34013 'Okehampton' at London Victoria with a Brighton train, 7th November, 1961.
78. 60039 'Sandwich' with a Newcastle - Kings Cross express at York, 10th June, 1962.
79. 45307 at Bolton Trinity Street with a Manchester Victoria - Blackpool South parcels train, 25th February, 1966.

76 78
77 79

80. 45336 at Kearsley with a Manchester Victoria - Blackpool South express, 26th February, 1966.
81. 48664 passes Stourton with a southbound freight, 22nd October, 1966.
82. 70026 'Polar Star' leaves Huddersfield and passes Red Doles Jnc. with a Stockport - Leeds City parcels train, 16th May, 1967.

83. 63675 with an eastbound freight from Colwick crosses the River Trent at Netherfield, 13th November, 1965.
84. 76063 east of Christchurch with a Bournemouth Central - Southampton Central train, 29th October, 1966.
85. 65795 north of Percy Main with coal empties for Rising Sun Colliery, 18th November, 1963.

65894 on 30th August, 1967

86. At the Bensham dive-under, Gateshead, returning from Stella.
87. Leaving Hylton Colliery for Sunderland South Dock.
88. Crossing the River Wear with coal from South Hetton Colliery to Stella South Power Station.

86
87 88

89. 65882 approaches Silksworth
with empty coal wagons from
South Dock, Sunderland, 31st
August, 1967.
90. Shunting at Stella South Power
Station, Blaydon, 22nd April, 1967.
91. The Howgill Incline to Haigh
Colliery from Whitehaven Harbour,
10th June, 1966.

92. 44715 below Lowca returning to Workington locomotive shed, 17th November, 1967.
93. 82034 approaches Morfa Mawddach with a Barmouth - Machynlleth train, 4th June, 1964.
94. 34108 'Axminster' on a Weymouth - Waterloo express at Poole, 29th October, 1966.

95. A light Bulleid Pacific approaches Totton, Southampton, 4th February, 1967.
96. 44822 near Reddish with a Newton Heath - Gowhole freight, 19th March 1966.
97. 76040 near Pentre Broughton, Wrexham, with a coal train for Brymbo Steel Works, 19th November, 1966.

98/99/100. 41835 working at Staveley Ironworks, 19th April, 1964.

101. 42455 approaches Wigan Central with a train from Irlam, 24th October, 1964.
102. 48062 with the Sandside-Carnforth freight east of Arnside, 12th January, 1968.
103. A southbound parcels train near Low Gill, 18th November, 1967.

104. A Class 8F 2.8.0 approaches Bolton-le-Sands with a northbound freight, 12th January, 1968.
105. 75077 at Lymington Jnc. with a Southampton-Weymouth train, 5th November, 1966.
106. Norwood, Gateshead, 1st September, 1967.

104
105 106

107. 45390 near Staveley, Cumbria, with the Windermere - Oxenholme pick-up, 14th September, 1967.
108. The 19.15 cattle train off Morpeth Dock, Birkenhead, 21st August, 1967.
109. 34052 'Lord Dowding' approaches Lymington Junction with a Weymouth - Waterloo express, 30th October, 1966.

108
107 109

110. 80154 on empty stock at Waterloo, 10th March, 1965.
111. 35003 'Royal Mail' leaves Southampton Central for Waterloo, 4th February, 1967.
112. 45104 comes off the Bury line at Castleton East Jnc. with flat wagons, as 48602 shunts the up sidings, 23rd August, 1967.

110
111 112

113. Bank Hall, Liverpool,
20th November, 1966.
114. 48769 pauses at Walsall station
with a train of empty coal wagons,
6th June, 1964.
115. 1648 at Llanglydwen with a
Whitland-Carmarthen train,
5th September, 1962.

Crumlin, 25th March, 1961.

116. 5264 with a northbound freight on the Ebbw Vale line.
117. 5698 crosses the viaduct east to west with a Pontypool Road - Aberdare High Level train.

118. A W.D. 2.8.0 and southbound freight cross the Forth Bridge from North Queensferry, 7th May, 1966.

119. 90436 approaches Wakefield Kirkgate with a Calder Valley freight, 29th February, 1964.
120. 90560 near Cumbernauld with a westbound freight, 13th June, 1965.
121. 90460 and 62070 on Retford (G.C.) locomotive shed, 8th June, 1964.

120
119 121

122. 63661 at Shireoaks East Jnc. with a westbound freight, 12th October, 1963.
123. 63636, 63701 and 62660 'Butler-Henderson' inside Gorton Works, 13th August, 1961.
124. 63611 left, and 63744 taking water at Mexborough locomotive shed, 18th June, 1961.
125. 63846 approaches Clowne (G.C.) with an eastbound freight, 18th April, 1964.

126/127/128. 43000, 62011,
North Blyth roundhouse
and coaling plant,
5th October, 1966.

129 130   St. Margaret's locomotive shed, Edinburgh, 13th June, 1965

129. 60052 'Prince Palatine' and its driving rods with 61354 receiving attention.
130. The driving wheels of 'Prince Palatine'.

131. 61191 and 80054
in St. Margaret's M.P.D.,
13th June, 1965.
132. A public house doorway in
Northwich, 9th February, 1968.
133. 42616 and 42689 on Low Moor
locomotive shed, Bradford,
24th August, 1967.

134. 35028 'Clan Line' in Clapham Cutting with a train for Bournemouth Central, 24th October, 1965.
135. 35025 'Brocklebank Line' with a Waterloo - Exeter Central train takes water at Salisbury, 31st May, 1964.

136. 44838 approaches Ditton Jnc., Widnes, with a westbound freight and passes an Andrew Barclay industrial locomotive working the adjacent works, 8th February, 1968.

137. 48476 waits just north of Tebay for banking assistance up to Shap Summit, 14th September, 1967.

138. 92166 runs beside the St. Helens Canal at Winwick Quay with a northbound freight, 15th July, 1967.

137

136 138

139. 47377 crosses the St. Helens Canal and approaches Pocket Nook Jnc., St. Helens, with a transfer freight from Sutton Junction, 7th June, 1966.

140. 45203 with a Bolton Trinity Street - Liverpool Exchange train passes over the Leeds and Liverpool Canal as it approaches Wigan Wallgate, 24th October, 1964.

141. 84026 shunts the yards at Bolton Trinity Street whilst 44664 waits to leave
with a train for Liverpool Exchange, 13th November, 1964.
142. 34087 '145 Squadron' at Bournemouth Central waits to leave
for Bournemouth West, with 76069 and 76064 at the opposite platform,
and 76014 on the centre road, 5th June, 1965.

143. 34102 'Lapford' at Earlsfield with a Southampton Central - Waterloo express, 30th December, 1966.
144. 76011 with a Bournemouth Central - Weymouth train
approaches Poole, 29th October, 1966.
145. 30055 near Rowfant with the East Grinstead - Three Bridges auto-train, 4th June, 1960.

146. 32348 at Ifield with a Horsham-Three Bridges freight, 12th May, 1961.
147. 61030 'Nyala' near Pudsey returning to Low Moor, Bradford, 24th August, 1967.
148. No. 20 'Shanklin' leaves Wroxall on a Ryde Pier Head-Ventnor train, 11th September, 1965.

146
147 148

149. Lamp-lighter on the down platform at Oxted, 6th January, 1965.
150. 92111 at Canning Street, Birkenhead returning to the locomotive shed, 21st August, 1967.

151. The north end of Stockton-on-Tees
station, 26th September, 1965.
152. 61275 takes on water at Nottingham Victoria
with a train for Sheffield Victoria as 43065 leaves
for Derby Friargate, 15th August, 1964.
153. 48744 takes on more than enough water
at Buxton M.P.D., 17th February, 1968.

154. 90621 and 63443 by the coaling plant at West Hartlepool M.P.D., 25th September, 1965.
155. 48439 passes Normanton locomotive shed with a southbound freight, 1st June, 1967.

154 155

156. 5084 'Reading Abbey' and 7316 at Plymouth Laira motive power depot, 29th October, 1961.
157. 6691 waits as 7219 takes on coal at Duffryn Yard M.P.D., Port Talbot, 10th March, 1963.

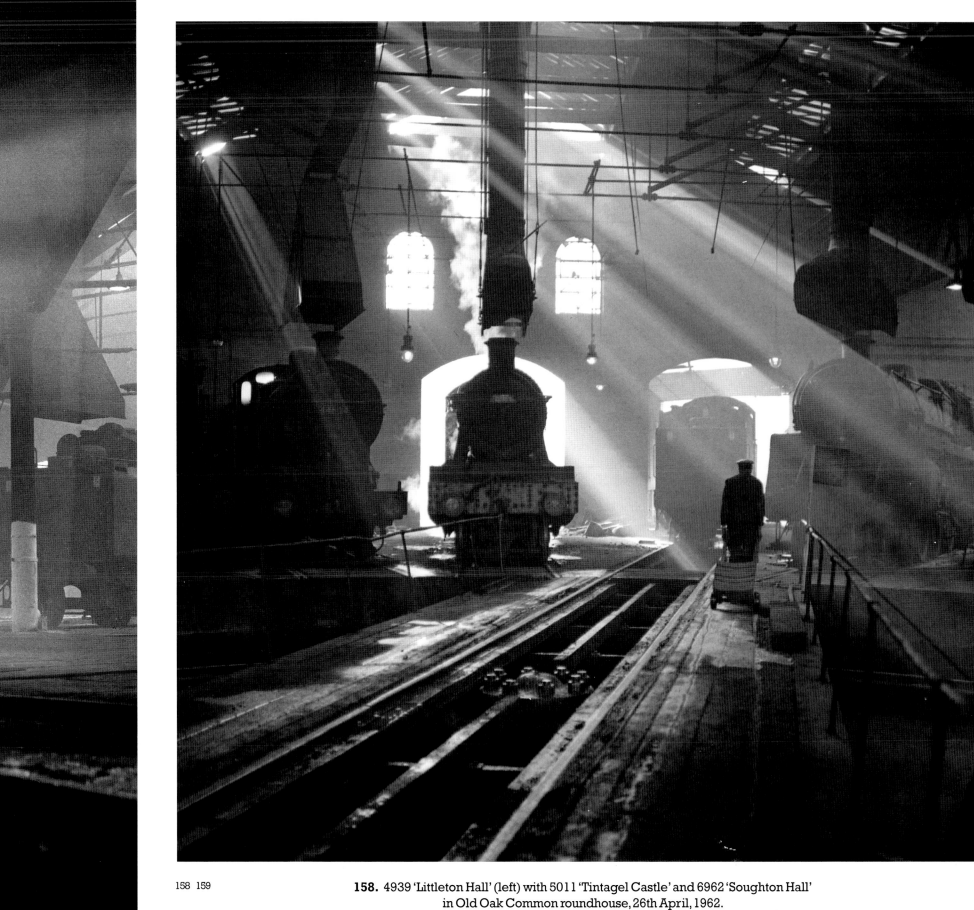

158. 4939 'Littleton Hall' (left) with 5011 'Tintagel Castle' and 6962 'Soughton Hall'
in Old Oak Common roundhouse, 26th April, 1962.
159. 44534 (left), 6910 'Gossington Hall', 44527 and 73003 in the roundhouse
at Barrow Road M.P.D., Bristol, 14th February, 1965.

Bristol Barrow Road locomotive depot, 14th February, 1965.

160. 5042 'Winchester Castle' and 8471 stand beside the ash pit.
161. 8403 (left) with 5042 and 8471 standing in the shed yard.

162 164
163

162. 4689 and brake van leave Stoke Gifford for Barrow Road, 20th February, 1965.
163. Permanent way train at Barlaston, 8th November, 1964.
164. 63458 propels its brake van from South Dock, Sunderland, past Seaton box, bound for South Hetton Colliery, 10th June, 1967.

165. 65331 passes Motherwell locomotive sheds with a southbound staff, tool and messing train, 3rd July, 1963.
166. 77004 at Conisbrough with an inspection saloon for Doncaster, 22nd May, 1963.
167. 61132 and westbound permanent way train near Lochgelly, 16th June, 1965.

168 170
169

168. 73150 leaves Gleneagles with a Dundee Tay Bridge-Glasgow Buchanan Street express, 17th June, 1964.
169. 9448 and permanent way train at Neath General, 26th May, 1961.
170. 92052 passes Heaton Lodge Jnc. with a westbound steel train, 16th May, 1967.

171. 48352, 48537 and 48222 on Royston locomotive sheds, 31st May, 1967.
172. 43027 by the iron ore conveyor at Haile Moor mine, 17th November, 1967.

43027 with its iron ore train, 17th November, 1967.

173. Passing Egremont.
174. Leaving Haile Moor for Workington.
175. At Whitehaven.

44829 and 43027 with
Workington-Beckermet Line
empties, 17th November, 1967.

176. Near Mirehouse.
177. Passing through Parton.
178. Approaching Moor Row.

176
177 178

179. 70025 'Western Star' climbs to Shap from Tebay at Birk Beck with a freight banked by 42251, 21st April, 1967.

180. 92076 approaches Ais Gill Summit with a Long Meg - Widnes anhydrite train, 21st April, 1967.
181. 92017 with a southbound freight at the same location, beneath Wild Baugh Fell, 15th September, 1967.

182. 45133 at Anfield with an Edge Hill - Alexandra Dock freight, 20th November, 1967.
183. 45110 and 48340 at Rose Grove M.P.D., 9th July, 1968.
184. 48732 with a permanent way train at Tamworth, 7th February, 1965.

183
182 184

185. 42981 passes Dukinfield Jnc. with a northbound freight, 19th March, 1966.
186. 44916 and 92022 double-head an Ellesmere Port - Neville Hill oil train
beside the River Tame at Dukinfield, 19th March, 1966.

187. 90148 passes Colwick East Junction with
westbound tankers, 13th November, 1965.
188. 48199 approaches Runcorn Bridge, above the River Mersey,
with tankers from Folly Lane works, 13th June, 1966.

187 188

The S.L.S. "Ashington Flyer" of 10th June, 1967.

189. 45562 'Alberta' crosses the River Blyth on Sleekburn Viaduct.
190. Crossing the River Wansbeck on Seaton Viaduct.

191. 48467 leaves Morpeth Dock with a transfer freight for Green Lane, Birkenhead, 21st August, 1967.
192. 48634 with Garston - Godley coal empties at Latchford as the
Finnish freighter 'Inari' passes on the Manchester Ship Canal, 19th April, 1968.

193. 46204 'Princess Louise' (left) with 46222 'Queen Mary' and 46223 'Princess Alice'
on Polmadie locomotive shed, Glasgow, 18th July, 1961.
194. 42251 receives close attention from enthusiasts on Low Moor shed, Bradford, 27th August, 1967.

195. 42189 with a King's Cross express leaves Halifax, 20th April, 1967.
196. 44694 leaves Halifax for Bradford Exchange with
a train from Bridlington, 26th August, 1967.

197. 45411 passes Salford with a train from Manchester Exchange to Glasgow Central, 2nd September, 1967.
198. 35012 'United States Line' approaches Vauxhall with a Waterloo - Bournemouth Central express, 10th March, 1965.
199. 63395 arrives at Norwood, Gateshead, with coal from South Hetton, 1st September, 1967.

200. 63395 with Norwood-South Hetton coal empties climbs Seaton bank, 31st August, 1967.
201. 63397 leaves West Hartlepool to collect a coal train from Blackhall Colliery, 27th September, 1965.

Northwich,
9th February, 1968.

202. Three 8F 2.8.0s by
Central Cabin.
203. 48631 crosses the
River Dane with a
freight for Hartford.

204
205

204. 80080 approaches Dovey Junction across the River Dovey with a Barmouth - Machynlleth train, 4th June, 1964.

205. 70022 'Tornado' crosses the Mersey south of Warrington with a Barrow/Morecombe - Euston express, 6th August, 1966.

206. 45305 takes the St. Helens line at Ince Moss, Wigan, with an inspection saloon, 23rd November, 1967.
207. 48036 with a permanent way train by Wigan Power Station, 19th November 1967.

208. 48767 at Ryecroft Jnc., Walsall, with Birchills-Hednesford coal empties, 16th November, 1963.
209. The 1 in 9 incline up to Sheep Pasture from just above Canal Wharf on the C.& H.P.R., 1st June, 1966.

Cromford and High Peak.

210. 47000 at Bolehill with the Sheep Pasture - Middleton Quarry freight, 1st June, 1966.
211. 47000 shunting Steeplehouse, Middleton Bottom, 1st June, 1966.
212. The bell and pointer signalling system at Middleton Top, 31st May, 1966.
213. 68006 leaves Middleton Top for Friden, 1st June, 1966.
214. 68012 leaves Parsley Hay for Middleton Top, 3rd March, 1967.

210 212 213
211   214

Great Rocks Dale, 13th May, 1967.

215. 48347 passes Tunstead Lime Works with a Buxton - Gowhole freight.
216. 48327 and a northbound lime train passes Tunstead Box.

215 216

217. 44775 approaches Ais Gill Summit with a southbound freight, 15th September, 1967.
218. A Class 9F 2.10.0 crosses Batty Moss Viaduct, Ribblehead, with a northbound freight, 29th August, 1967.

219. 41224 leaves Lymington Town station with a Brockenhurst - Lymington Pier train.
220. 41224 runs round its train at Lymington Pier later the same day, 6th November, 1966.

221. Signal lamp inspection at Barnstaple Junction station, 2nd June, 1964.
222. 31551 propels its auto-train for Three Bridges away from East Grinstead, 17th December, 1961.
223. Signalman Peter Suttie, proud of his Shore Road (Stirling East) signal box, 20th July, 1962.

224. 82022 with empty stock for Waterloo at Clapham Junction, 3rd November, 1965.

225. 48711 approaches Lancaster
Castle station with a southbound freight,
20th June, 1964.
226. 70020 'Mercury' leaves Worcester
Shrub Hill with the Hereford portion
of the "Cathedrals Express",
26th July, 1961.
227. 43139 at Langholm on the
last day of service from Carlisle,
13th June, 1964.

228. 45156 'Ayshire Yeomanry' at Manchester Victoria on 4th August 1968,

… "Farewell to Steam" …